Sounds All Around

Diana Menefy

photographs by Adam Pryor

Contents

Page 2   Sound Waves

Page 3   Decibels

Page 4   Sounds People Make

Page 6   Sounds Machines Make

Page 8   Hard-to-hear Sounds

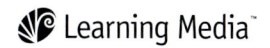

Sound Waves

Sound is felt by the ear when sound waves hit the eardrum. Sounds can be measured.

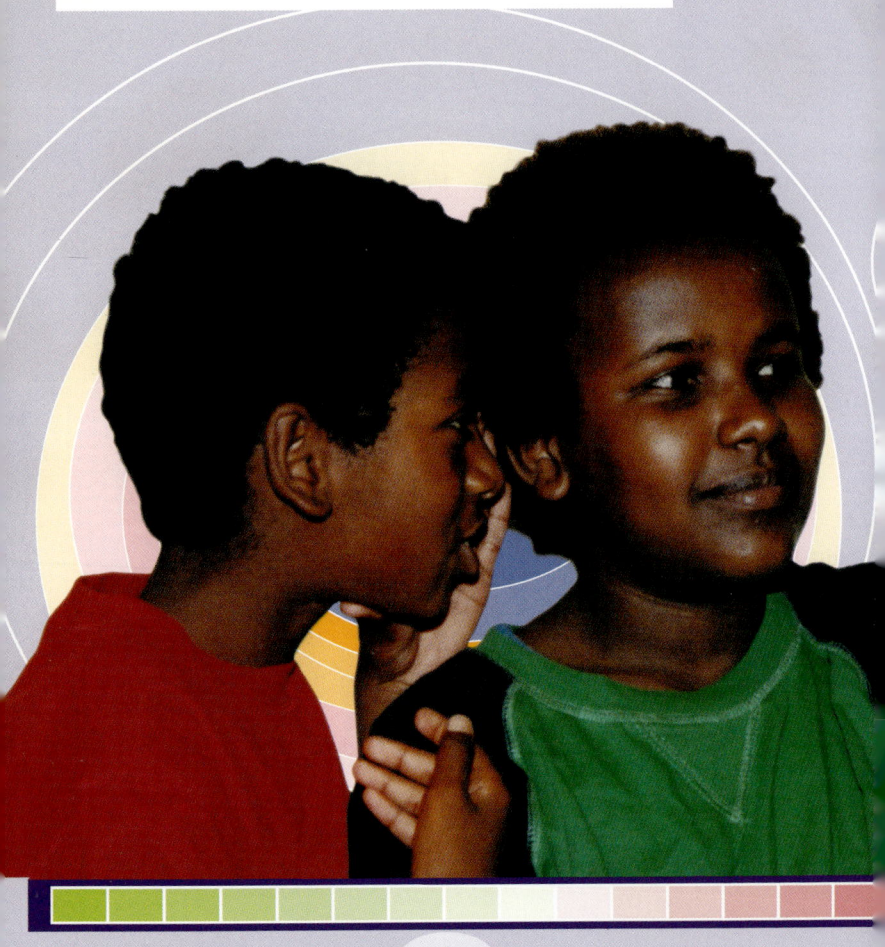

Decibels

Sounds are measured in decibels. The sound of a pin dropping measures about 1 decibel. The sound of wind in the leaves on a tree measures about 10 decibels.

Sounds People Make

The sounds of two people talking measure 65 decibels.
The sounds in a classroom of twenty children all talking measure about 80 decibels.
That's almost as much as a personal tape or CD player.

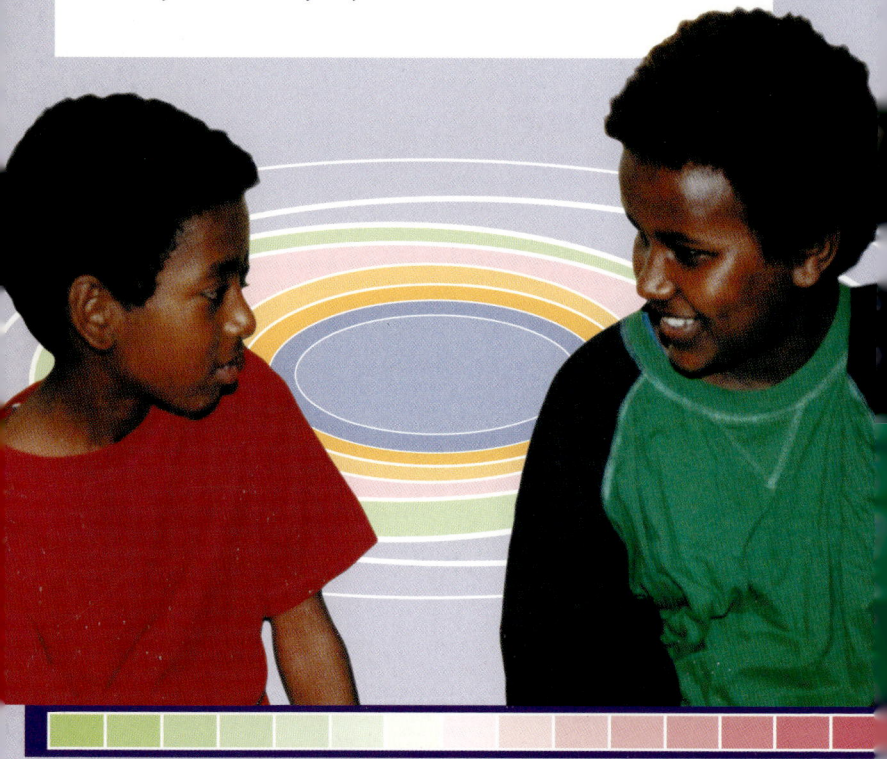

A personal tape or CD player
with the volume turned to high
can measure between
105 and 120 decibels.
At that volume,
it will be damaging your eardrums!
Keep the volume low.

Sounds Machines Make

The sound inside a subway when a train speeds past can measure
up to 100 decibels.
It's noisy down there!
People need to wear earmuffs to muffle the sound when the noise measures
85 decibels or more.
That's so that they don't
damage their eardrums.

When sounds measure about
130 decibels, the ear begins to hurt.
Very loud sounds can tear the eardrum
and make it bleed.
A jet taking off measures 150 decibels.
That's why the ground controller
wears special earmuffs.

Hard-to-hear Sounds

The quietest sound that the ear can hear is different for each person.
Some people can hear a sound that measures −10 decibels.
For some people, the hardest sound of all to hear is

"It's time to get up!"